THE SKELETON AND MUSCLES

Steve Parker

HODDER
Wayland

an imprint of Hodder Children's Books

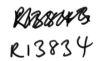

Titles in the series:
The Brain and Nervous System • Digestion
The Heart, Lungs and Blood • Reproduction
The Senses • The Skeleton and Muscles

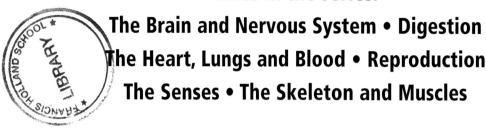

Produced by Monkey Puzzle Media Ltd
Gissing's Farm, Fressingfield, Suffolk IP21 5SH, UK

Text copyright © 2003 Steve Parker
Series copyright © 2003 Hodder Wayland
First published in 2003 by Hodder Wayland
an imprint of Hodder Children's Books
Reprinted in 2003

Commissioning Editor: Victoria Brooker
Book Editor: Nicola Edwards
Design: Jane Hawkins
Picture Research: Sally Cole
Artwork: Alex Pang
Consultant: Dr Trish Groves

British Library Cataloguing in Publication Data
Parker, Steve, 1952-
  The skeleton and muscles. – (Our bodies)
  1. Human skeleton – Juvenile literature
  2. Musculoskeletal system – Juvenile literature
  I.Title
  612.7

ISBN 07502 3672 8

Printed and bound in China

Hodder Children's Books
A division of Hodder Headline Limited
338 Euston Road, London NW1 3BH

Picture Acknowledgements
Alamy 9, 13, 34–35; Corbis 5 (Robbie Jack), 30 (Steve Prezant); Corbis Digital Stock *front cover* inset, 37 right; Digital Vision 1, 23 top, 29, 40; FLPA 35 (Chris Mattison); Getty Images *front cover* main image (Taxi), 33 bottom (Stone), 39 (Taxi), 45 (The Image Bank); ImageState 24, 31, 37 left; Panos 11; Robert Harding Picture Library 7, 23 bottom (Tony Gervis); Science Photo Library 4 (Simon Fraser), 14 (NASA), 15 (Athenais, ISM), 17, 19 bottom (Pr. S Cinti/CNRI), 20 (BSIP Ducloux), 21 (Astrid & Hanns-Frider Michler), 26 (Deep Light Productions), 38 (Salisbury District Hospital), 44 (Princess Margaret Rose Hospital); Wellcome Trust 43.

CONTENTS

Supporting parts

Many parts of the body are soft and flexible – the nerves and brain, heart and blood vessels, stomach and intestines are all squishy and bendy. To stop the body sagging onto the floor like a heap of jelly, it is held up by a very strong set of supporting parts, called bones. Each bone is rigid and strong, and all the bones together form the body's inner framework, which allows us to stand tall and move about.

BETWEEN BONES

Bones are not separate parts, distant from each other and scattered around the body. They are linked together at joints, of many different sizes and designs. Joints hold the bones together so they do not come apart but do let them move in relation to each other. Joints also reduce wear and tear, stopping the ends of the bones rubbing and scraping against each other as they move to and fro.

The body's inner supporting framework, called the skeleton, shows up clearly in this whole-body scan as pale white-mauve bones of many sizes and shapes.

PULLING BONES

Bones cannot move by themselves. They are moved by muscles. The body has hundreds of muscles, ranging from large and powerful ones, like those in the hips and upper legs, to tiny and delicate muscles deep inside the ear. Muscles have one main task: to get shorter, or contract. Most muscles are firmly joined to bones. As a muscle contracts, it pulls on the bones and moves them nearer to each other. This moves body parts, from

Dancers train to ensure their muscles are strong and their joints are flexible or supple, so that they can take up hundreds of different body positions.

a finger or toe to a whole arm or leg, or the neck and back.

The muscles, bones and joints make up the musculo-skeletal system. This system supports us and enables us to move around, jump, run, lift and pull objects. It also allows us to smile, shout, clap and even breathe.

THE SKELETON

In the middle

If you were to take away a body's skin, nerves, blood vessels, muscles, guts and other soft parts, the last items left, in the middle of the body, would be the bones. The adult human body has a total of 206 bones, and together, they are known as the skeleton. Bones make up about one-sixth of the body's total weight.

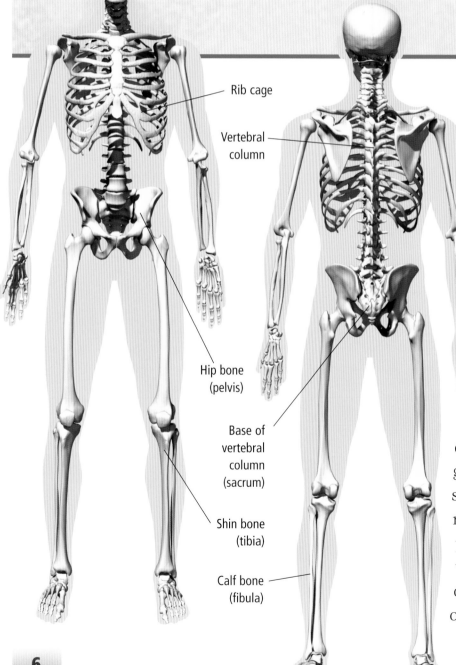

Rib cage

Vertebral column

Hip bone (pelvis)

Base of vertebral column (sacrum)

Shin bone (tibia)

Calf bone (fibula)

Seen from the rear, the skeleton looks different from the front view, especially the skull and vertebral column of backbones.

BUSY BONES

Old bones and skeletons, in museums and exhibitions, usually look dry, dull, whitened, flaking and brittle. But inside the body, living bones are quite different. They are greyish and damp-looking, slightly bendy, and very much alive. Like other body parts, they have blood vessels and nerve connections. They even change shape slowly and

ANIMAL VERSUS HUMAN

Sharks are powerful hunters of the open ocean. Like us, they have a skeleton – yet there is not a single bone in a shark's body. Its skeleton is made entirely of cartilage (gristle) rather than bone.

The shark has ribs and many other skeletal parts – but made of cartilage, not bone.

slightly through life, in response to stresses and strains on the body, and its patterns of movement. This can happen when someone changes from one sport or activity to another, for example, switching from hurdling to horse-riding.

NAMES OF BONES

Every bone has a scientific or medical name. In fact, every part of every bone – each lump or bump, hollow or curve – has its own scientific name. Many bones also have more ordinary, everyday names. Examples are the kneecap, which is known scientifically as the patella, and the cheek bone, called the zygomatic bone. The 'funny bone' is not a whole bone; rather it is formed by the elbow ends of the long bones called the humerus in the upper arm, and the ulna in the forearm.

CARTILAGE

Bone is the skeleton's main structural substance, and it is very strong. But the body has another structural substance called cartilage or 'gristle'. Cartilage is similar in many ways to bone, but it is slightly softer and bendier. With bone, it forms parts of the skeleton, especially in the ribs in the chest. Cartilage also covers the ends of bones in joints and makes up several structural parts of the body, such as the nose and ears.

weblinks

To find out more about the skeleton, go to: www.waylinks.co.uk/series/ourbodies/skelandmus

Try this!

If you press your nose and tweak your ear, they bend. They have cartilage inside, to support them and give them shape. If they were bone, they would be very stiff indeed. Knocked hard, they might snap off!

INSIDE BONES

Layer upon layer

A bone is like a piece of wood – light, tough, hard, strong, and slightly bendy. But, unlike wood, bone is not the same all the way through. Most bones have three layers, one inside the other.

Outer covering (periosteum)

Blood supply to bone

A typical bone has three main layers – a hard outer shell or casing of compact bone, a spongy layer under this, and a centre of jelly-like marrow.

End or head of bone

Compact (hard) bone

Cancellous (spongy) bone

Marrow and blood vessels

Main length or shaft of bone

ON THE OUTSIDE

The outer layer is known as compact or hard bone. It provides most of the toughness and strength. Compact bone is made of thousands of tiny rod-shaped parts called osteons, packed together like drinking straws in a box. Each osteon is thinner than a human hair and consists of layers of hard mineral crystals.

MICRO-BODY

In each osteon, crystals and fibres are arranged in wider and wider layers, like smaller tubes inside larger tubes. In the hole along the middle are microscopic blood vessels and a tiny nerve.

The crystals, mainly calcium, phosphate and carbonate, are scattered among bundles of thread-like fibres of another substance, the protein collagen.

IN THE MIDDLE

Inside compact bone is a layer of cancellous or spongy bone. It is a mass of collagen fibres and mineral crystals, like compact bone, but it also contains thousands of small, bubble-like holes. Cancellous bone is quite strong, and also very light. It helps to reduce the weight of the whole bone and allows it to be slightly flexible, so that under great stress, it is more likely to bend rather than snap.

ON THE INSIDE

Most bones have a soft, jelly-like centre, called bone marrow. This is very active, making microscopic new red and white blood cells for the whole body's blood system, to replace blood cells which naturally wear out and die. Bone marrow is very busy. Every second, the marrow in the body's bones makes two million new red cells, and tens of thousands of new white cells.

ANIMAL VERSUS HUMAN

We have our bones on the inside. Some animals have bone on the outside too. Tortoises, armadillos and pangolins have body coverings made of bony plates, for protection. The bone is covered by another tough substance, horn.

The giant tortoise's shell has bony plates covered by plates of tough, hard horn.

THE GROWING SKELETON

THE UNBORN BABY

Like other body parts, the bones of an unborn baby start to develop when it is tiny, hardly larger than your thumb. But at this very early stage, the 'bones' are not actually made of bone. Their shapes form first as softer, bendier cartilage. Over months in the womb, and then in the years following birth, this cartilage gradually develops mineral crystals and hardens into true bone. This process is called ossification.

STAGES OF GROWTH

The skeleton begins to appear in the form of cartilage, by about the third week after a human body starts to

The changing size and proportions of the growing body are based on the developing skeleton. As a child grows, parts of the skeleton which first formed as cartilage become turned into bone. One of the main changes is the formation of mineral crystals such as calcium phosphate, which make the bone harder but less bendy.

develop from the tiny fertilized egg inside its mother's womb. After another five weeks (which is still seven months before birth), some of this cartilage starts to harden into true bone, as the skeleton itself continues to grow in size. This process happens at different rates in different areas of the body. When a baby is born, its skull and backbone are quite well formed and hardened into bone, although they are still growing. The wrist and ankle 'bones' have much less bone – they are still mainly cartilage. The long bones in the arms and legs will not be completely bone until 15-18 years of age, when the person reaches full adult height.

BONE PROBLEMS

Bones need minerals and other substances to become tough and hard. One important substance is vitamin D. If this is lacking in a person's diet, the bone cannot harden fully. It may stay soft and grow in the wrong shape. If this happens during childhood, as the skeleton is growing, it is known as rickets. It can cause problems such as bent or 'bowed' legs. The same problem in adults is known as osteomalacia.

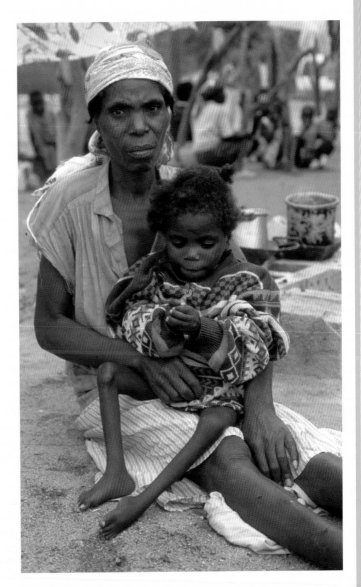

Lack of healthy food makes the bones weak, so they cannot support the body and do not grow in the usual shape.

ANIMAL VERSUS HUMAN

Some animal skeletons develop very fast. A mouse's is fully grown by four weeks! Other animal skeletons never stop developing. A tortoise or crocodile may still be growing at 80 years old – although more slowly than when it was younger.

BONES OF THE SKULL AND FACE

Protection

The main bones inside the head are called the skull and lower jaw. The complicated shape of the skull protects five of the body's most delicate parts – the eyes, ears and brain. The two eyes are set in deep bowls called orbits, in the front of the skull. The tiny inner parts of each ear are inside a chamber within the thickness of the side of the skull, in the temporal bone. And the brain is protected by the curved dome over the top, known as the cranium.

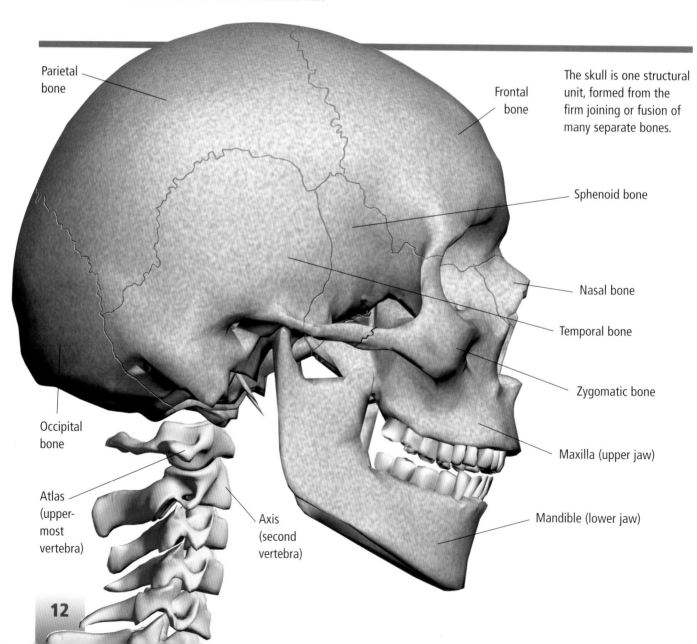

Parietal bone

Frontal bone

The skull is one structural unit, formed from the firm joining or fusion of many separate bones.

Sphenoid bone

Nasal bone

Temporal bone

Zygomatic bone

Occipital bone

Maxilla (upper jaw)

Atlas (upper-most vertebra)

Axis (second vertebra)

Mandible (lower jaw)

The proportions of the skull bone determine the overall shape of the face, from wide to narrow.

THE SMALLEST BONES

The human skull is made of 21 bones linked firmly at suture joints (see page 32). There are seven other bones in the head, too. Six of the bones (three deep inside each ear) are the smallest bones of the entire body. They are called the hammer, anvil and stirrup: the stirrup is hardly larger than this letter U. These bones help us to hear, passing sound vibrations from the eardrum to the innermost ear. The seventh bone is one of the body's strongest – the lower jaw, or mandible. It is moved by muscles that are, for their relative size, some of the body's most powerful. They are the temporalis in front of the ear, and the masseter under the cheek bone. These are the muscles we use to bite and chew.

Top Tips

In risky sports and activities, a helmet or hard-hat or head-guard protects not only your skull, but your eyes and ears – and your brain! In some high-speed activities, like skiing and cycling, you cannot take part unless you are wearing some form of protection for your head.

Try this!

Speak loudly as normal, then hold your nose and speak again. Your voice sounds different. Normally, sounds pass through the nose, and this is linked to air chambers called sinuses, inside the bones of your face. The sounds fill these air chambers and make your voice louder and clearer. If you hold your nose, air cannot pass this way.

HEALTHY BONES

Keeping fit

The body stays fitter, healthier and in better shape, if it keeps active. This is true of all body parts, including bones. Every day, we can make sure that our bones and other body parts have the best chance of staying strong and healthy.

EATING AND BONES

Bones contain minerals such as calcium and phosphate. To keep our bones healthy, we need to eat plenty of these minerals, in a range of foods such as milk, dairy products, meat, fish and fresh fruits and vegetables. In an emergency, when food is lacking, the body can take some of the minerals out of the bones, for more urgent needs elsewhere. But this weakens the bones, and the minerals need to be replaced quickly.

ACTIVITY AND BONES

If muscles are not used regularly, they become weak and gradually waste away. The same happens to bones. They are designed to cope with a certain amount of stress and strain during movement. Most kinds of activity keep bones strong and tough, as well as benefiting other body parts, like the heart and lungs.

Astronauts take regular exercise, otherwise the weightless conditions of space would weaken their bones and muscles.

Activities range from energetic sports such as football and tennis, to swimming, jogging and even brisk walking. Doing the opposite – sitting and lying down for long periods of time – means that bones lose their strength, and become at greater risk from breaks or other injuries.

HELPING BONES

Bones are tough, but sometimes they are put under so much strain that they crack or even break. This usually happens when the body is moving fast and then stops suddenly – such as in a road accident, a fall or a collision in high-speed sport. So it's important to wear protective clothing and equipment. A helmet protects the skull in the head. Shoulder pads cover the collar bones. Elbow and knee guards protect the bone ends and joints there. In football, shin pads cover the front of the lower leg, which is at risk from the accidental kicks of other players.

This X-ray shows a break (see upper left) in the fibula or calf bone, in the lower leg just above the ankle.

weblinks

To find out more about healthy bones, go to:
www.waylinks.co.uk/series/ourbodies/skelandmus

Try this!

Feel where bones are near the surface of the body. They form hard bumps just under the skin. Bones in these places are at risk of cracks or breaks when knocked hard, because they are not covered by softer parts like muscles or fat, which absorb the blow. Examples include the shin, ankle, elbow and collar area.

THE MUSCLE SYSTEM

Making movements

Muscles do almost nothing except become shorter, or contract, and then relax and become longer again. By doing this, they make every movement of the body. This includes not only the movements we see on the outside, such as walking, running and jumping. It also includes movements inside the body, like swallowing, breathing and pumping blood.

Biceps brachi

Triceps brachi

Flexors for fingers

Extensors for fingers

Gracilis

Gluteus maximus

Biceps femoris

Rectus femoris

Tibialis anterior

Gastrocnemius

Extensors for toes

Flexors for toes

Some of the main superficial or outermost muscles of the body.

MUSCLES AND BONES

The body has about 640 skeletal muscles. These are the muscles which are mainly joined to the bones of the skeleton. Skeletal muscles pull bones to move the body about. Skeletal muscles are also called voluntary muscles, because we can control them in a voluntary way, or at will, by thoughts and decisions. And they are known as striped muscles, because under the microscope, they have a pattern of tiny light and dark stripes. Other kinds of muscle, which are not voluntary and not striped, are shown on the next pages.

NAMES AND SHAPES

We often think of a muscle as long, bulging in the middle, and thinner at each end where it attaches to a bone. This is true for many muscles in the arms and legs. But there are plenty of other shapes and designs of muscles. Sometimes a muscle's name is taken from its shape or its connections with bones. The deltoid muscle in the shoulder has three sides, like a triangle ('delta' means triangle-shaped). The triceps muscle in the arm is named because it is Y-shaped with three ends, which are called 'heads' in muscles ('tri' means 3, 'ceph' means head).

MICRO-BODY

Skeletal or striped muscle shows its dark and light bands, or striations, under the microscope. As it gets shorter, the lighter bands become narrower.

The striations (stripes) of skeletal muscle are formed by the overlapping of long, thin substances within them, especially actin and myosin.

Different types

Most of the muscles in the body are skeletal muscles (see previous page). They form about two-fifths of the body's whole weight. They pull on bones and move the body about, and we can control them at will. But the body has two other kinds of muscle, known as visceral and cardiac muscle.

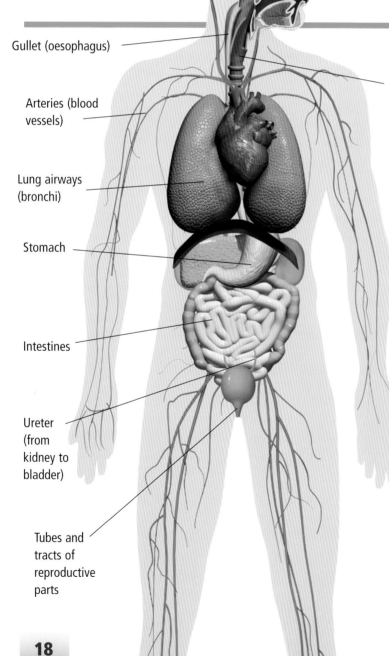

Gullet (oesophagus)

Windpipe (trachea)

Arteries (blood vessels)

Lung airways (bronchi)

Stomach

Intestines

Ureter (from kidney to bladder)

Tubes and tracts of reproductive parts

MUSCLES FOR THE INSIDES

Visceral muscle is found mainly as layers in the walls or coverings of inner body parts like the stomach and intestines, blood vessels, and air tubes in the lungs. It also forms bag-like containers, such as in the bladder. Visceral muscle is sometimes called smooth muscle because, under the microscope, it does not have tiny stripes like skeletal muscle. It looks smooth and flat. Visceral muscle is also known as involuntary muscle. This is because its works automatically, on its own, and we cannot affect it at will, by thinking.

Smooth (visceral or involuntary) muscle is found in many body parts, including the walls of blood vessels that branch throughout the body.

Visceral muscles are not joined to bones. They work by contracting in a wave-like fashion along their length. In a tube, this pushes the contents along. An example is in the intestine (gut), where food is pushed and squeezed along as it is digested. The wave-like squeezing motion is known as peristalsis.

Gullet

Rugae (wrinkled inner lining)

Middle muscle layer (circular)

Innermost muscle layer (oblique)

Outer muscle layer (longitudinal)

Outer covering

The stomach wall contains several layers of smooth muscle, with their fibres arranged in different directions, to allow a wide range of squeezing movements.

HEART MUSCLE

The heart is almost all muscle – a special type called cardiac muscle or myocardium. Skeletal muscles get tired or fatigued if we use them too much. Heart muscle never fatigues – which is fortunate, because it has to contract and pump blood every second, to keep the body alive.

— weblinks▶ —
To find out more about the smooth muscles, go to:
www.waylinks.co.uk/series/ourbodies/skelandmus

MICRO-BODY

Under a microscope, visceral muscle lacks the thin stripes or bands of skeletal muscle. Also it can contract for longer periods than skeletal muscle, without getting tired.

Smooth or visceral muscle, magnified 3760 times

Try this!

Swallow hard while touching your neck to feel the muscles of your gullet (oesophagus), inside your neck. They contract or squeeze like a wave, to push swallowed items down into your stomach.

TENDONS

Anchored onto bones

A bulging muscle does not usually join directly to a bone. In most cases, the muscle end tapers into a tough, rope-like, narrower tendon. This is the part which is firmly stuck or anchored onto the bone. Tendons are pale because they have much less blood in them than muscles. They are made mainly of string-like fibres of the body substance collagen (which is also found in bones and in the skin).

LIVING GLUE

At the muscle end, the tendon is joined mainly to the outer layer or 'skin' around the muscle, known as the epimysium. At the bone end, it is joined to a similar outer 'skin' around the bone, called the periosteum. Both of these joins are very strong. It takes great force to pull a tendon from its bone or muscle, or to stretch it so that it tears. If this happens, we often call it a 'strained muscle' or 'torn muscle' when, in fact, it's really the tendon which is injured.

This computer-coloured scan shows an achilles tendon above the heel which was put under excessive strain, resulting in a tear (arrowed).

LONG TENDONS

Some muscles have more than one 'end'. When you curl up your toes, you use a muscle in the front of the lower leg, called an extensor. It has one tendon at its upper end. But at the lower end it branches into three parts, each with a tendon. The three tendons run down through the ankle, and along the top of the foot, to pull on the tops of the toes and make them curl up.

Tendons are pale in colour, partly because they contain little blood compared to well-supplied, blood-rich body parts such as muscles.

Try this!

Stand up straight, then bend your knees to crouch slightly. Feel two large tendons just above the back of your knee, called hamstring tendons, take the strain. Also feel the body's largest tendon, just above the heel, called the calcaneal or achilles tendon.

MICRO-BODY

This microscope view of a tendon shows its strong, stringy fibres, with few blood vessels or nerves. The small blood supply means an injured tendon usually takes a long time to heal.

Muscle fibres

A big muscle contains thousands of long, thin parts called muscle fibres (myofibres). Each one of these is thinner than a human hair. In most muscles the fibres are about three or four centimetres in length, but in a long muscle, they may be 30 centimetres long. The muscle fibres are wrapped in bundles known as fascicles, and the whole muscle is wrapped in a strong outer layer or 'skin' called the epimysium (see page 20).

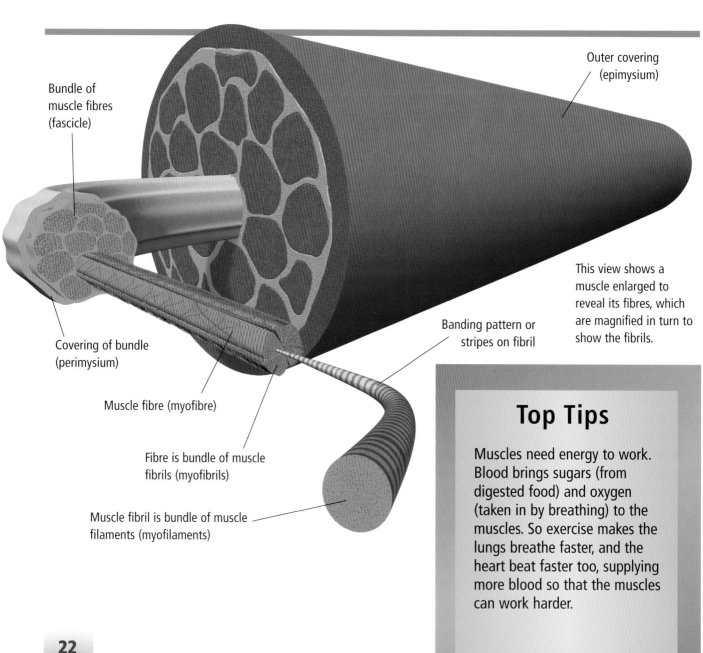

Outer covering (epimysium)

Bundle of muscle fibres (fascicle)

Covering of bundle (perimysium)

Muscle fibre (myofibre)

Fibre is bundle of muscle fibrils (myofibrils)

Muscle fibril is bundle of muscle filaments (myofilaments)

Banding pattern or stripes on fibril

This view shows a muscle enlarged to reveal its fibres, which are magnified in turn to show the fibrils.

Top Tips

Muscles need energy to work. Blood brings sugars (from digested food) and oxygen (taken in by breathing) to the muscles. So exercise makes the lungs breathe faster, and the heart beat faster too, supplying more blood so that the muscles can work harder.

PARTS THAT PULL

A single muscle fibre contains a bundle of even thinner parts, known as muscle fibrils (myofibrils). These have light and dark patches that line up across many fibrils, to give a striped or banded appearance (see page 17). The fibrils are made of two body substances, or proteins, known as actin and myosin. These are long and thin and lie alongside each other, partly overlapping. To make the muscle pull, the actins and myosins slide past each other, so the whole fibril becomes shorter. Most muscles can contract to about two-thirds their length, bulging fatter as they do so.

An adult male gorilla is over one-half muscle.

ANIMAL VERSUS HUMAN

Some animals have far more muscle in their bodies, for their size, than we do. The gorilla is especially strong. It does not have extra muscles compared to us, but each muscle is bigger than the same muscle in a person.

weblinks

To find out more about muscle fibres, go to:
www.waylinks.co.uk/series/ourbodies/skelandmus

In a muscle fibril, actins and myosins move past each other, like people pulling hand-over-hand on a rope.

MAKING MOVEMENTS

WORKING TOGETHER

Very few movements in the body use just one muscle. If you bend your elbow, the main muscle involved is the biceps. You can see it bulging in the top of your upper arm. But under this are two more muscles, the coraco-brachialis near the shoulder, and the brachialis lower down towards the elbow. These two help the biceps. At the same time other muscles become tense all down your arm, from shoulder to wrist. Otherwise your shoulder would tilt forwards, and your wrist and hand would go floppy. The 'simple' movement of bending your elbow involves at least 20 muscles!

Hundreds of muscles all over the body are used when dancing to produce graceful, delicately controlled motions.

Try this!

Whirl your arm around at the shoulder like a windmill, and feel the wide range of movements at this joint. It involves at least 50 muscles, which pull or steady the arm in different ways as it goes around in a circle.

Deltoid

Pectoralis major

Latissimus dorsi

Biceps brachi

The shoulder is surrounded and stabilized by many muscles, which move the upper arm and also the elbow.

PULL, NOT PUSH

To straighten your elbow, you do not use the biceps again. A muscle can only pull. It cannot forcefully push to move bones farther apart. The elbow is straightened by the triceps muscle in the underside of your upper arm. As the triceps shortens, the biceps becomes relaxed or floppy, and the movement stretches it longer. So the biceps moves the elbow one way, and the triceps moves it back again. These two muscles are called opposing or antagonistic partners. Straightening the elbow, like bending it, uses a host of other muscles from the shoulder down to the wrist. Nearly all body movements are like this. They use teams of muscles, rather than just one or two.

Twin heads (upper ends) of biceps brachi

Biceps brachi

Triceps brachi

The triceps and biceps are opposing muscle partners. The biceps is so called because it has two ends, or heads, while the triceps has three.

25

CONTROLLING MUSCLES

Nerve messages

Skeletal or voluntary muscles do not move on their own. Otherwise our body actions would be very random, jerky and clumsy! They are controlled by the brain. It sends out messages along nerves, which are like bendy wires that branch throughout the body. Nerve messages are tiny pulses of electricity. The nerve end passes the messages into the muscle fibres, to make these contract. Nerve messages travel very fast, at 100 metres per second or more. So a message's journey, from brain to muscle, takes a fraction of a second.

The tiny electrical signals made by active muscles are displayed by an electromyograph (EMG) machine.

MOVEMENTS AND THE BRAIN

The nerve messages to muscles come from several parts of the brain. The main one is the movement centre or motor cortex. This is a strip on the outside of the brain, from the top of the head, down towards the ear. It's the place where we think about, and decide to make or stop, voluntary movements.

Try this!

Try to pat your head with one hand, and rub circles on your stomach with the other, at the same time. It's quite difficult at first because it is an unnatural movement that we rarely do. But keep practising. The brain gradually learns to move the muscles in the right way.

Premotor cortex

Main part of brain (cerebrum)

Motor cortex

Cerebellum

Spinal cord

After leaving the motor cortex, the nerve messages pass through another part of the brain, before they leave along nerves. This is the small, wrinkled cerebellum, at the brain's lower rear.

The cerebellum 'fills in the details' of exactly which muscles should contract, and when, and by how much. We are not usually aware of this. We decide in the motor cortex to make a movement, then go on to other thoughts. The cerebellum takes care of the details. It makes our movements smooth, practised and coordinated – until we have to learn new ones, like playing a piano, rollerblading or windsurfing.

weblinks

To find out more about controlling muscles, go to:
www.waylinks.co.uk/series/ourbodies/skelandmus

Motor nerve

Terminal branches of motor nerve fibre

Terminal of motor nerve fibre

Nerve-muscle junction (motor end plate)

Muscle fibres

Surface of muscle fibre

Synapse (link)

Nerve messages from parts of the brain (top) travel along nerves to muscles (left), where the nerve endings are embedded in the hair-fine muscle fibres (bottom).

MICRO-BODY

The motor end plate is a spider-like, microscopic part that joins a nerve end to a muscle. It passes the nerve messages into the muscle fibres, to make them contract.

MUSCLES OF THE FACE AND HEAD

Unusual and useful

Under the skin of the face, there are about 50 muscles. They are among the most unusual and useful in the body. They are unusual because some of them are not joined to bones at each end. They are joined to each other, by straps of fibres. They form a complex web or network of muscles, which can move in hundreds of different ways. These muscles give us a vast range of facial expressions, so we can communicate our thoughts and feelings to other people, without a sound.

Frontalis

Orbicularis oculi

Platysma

Levator labii

Zygomaticus major

Risorius

Orbicularis oris (lips)

Depressor labii

Many facial muscles are joined to other muscles rather than to bones.

Try this!

Make various faces in a mirror, to see how your facial muscles work. Pull your mouth very wide, using the risorius muscle in each cheek. Then curl the corners of your mouth up for a smile, out wider for a grin, and down for a nervous frown.

OPEN AND SHUT

Each eyelid is a four-part, circle-shaped muscle called the orbicularis oculi. It has a large opening in the middle – which we see through! When this muscle contracts, the upper and lower parts come together, to close the opening. This is how we blink our eyelids and shut our eyes. There is a similar but larger circle-like muscle in the lips, the orbicularis oris. When it contracts, the mouth closes.

BENDIEST MUSCLE

The body's most bendy muscle is just behind the lips. It's the tongue. In fact a tongue has 12 separate muscles. It is much longer in total, than the part you can see. It is anchored at its lower end, down in the throat and neck region. The tongue can twist and curve into many shapes, from short and wide to long and thin. Using the tongue we can eat, lick, swallow, suck, speak, and even whistle.

ANIMAL VERSUS HUMAN

Lizards do not seem to laugh or frown. In fact, they cannot, even if they wanted. They have fewer and less complicated muscles in their faces. Only a few animals can make lots of facial expressions, mainly monkeys and apes.

weblinks

To find out more about the muscles of the face and head, go to: www.waylinks.co.uk/series/ourbodies/skelandmus

The chimp's lips are very flexible, able to make many facial expressions as well as to gather small food items.

BONE AND MUSCLE DISORDERS

Injuries

Bones and muscles are the body's most physical parts, carrying out endless movements, often under stress and strain. Sometimes the stress becomes too much, and something 'snaps'.

A fracture is a crack, split or complete break in a bone. As a bone heals after a break or fracture, microscopic cells in the bone form new fibres and mineral crystals. After a few months, the break is hardly visible. A dislocation is where two bones in a joint, which are supposed to be held next to each other, come away from each other. A sprained joint is when the bones move farther than they should in relation to each other, stretching or tearing the parts around, like muscles and ligaments. (see page 33.)

TREATMENT

The usual treatment for these injuries is for a doctor to check that all parts are back in their correct places, with an operation if necessary. This is followed by resting the affected part, then very gradual movements and gentle exercises.

Crutches help to take the weight off an injured leg while it is exercised to keep it mobile.

WASTED MUSCLES

Compared to most other body parts, muscles do not suffer from many diseases. In paralysis, a body part cannot be moved. This is more often due to a problem in the brain or nerves that control a muscle, rather than in the muscle itself. In muscular dystrophy, the muscle fibres do not work properly because of a problem in the way they use the mineral calcium, which helps to control their contraction. The muscles become weak and wasted.

WEAK BONES

Because bones are the body's support system, any problem which reduces their strength can have widespread effects. In osteoporosis, bones lose their hard mineral structure and become weak, brittle and crumbly. This condition tends to affect older women because their bodies have stopped producing certain natural body chemicals, or hormones, which help to keep bones strong. Osteoporosis is also made more likely by smoking, unhealthy eating with not enough vitamins and minerals, and lack of exercise. It can often be treated by tablets, and by gradual activity to strengthen the bones again.

weblinks

To find out more about bone and muscle disorders, go to:
www.waylinks.co.uk/series/ourbodies/skelandmus

Top Tips

In some sports and activities, special joint supports or strappings are recommended. These give extra support to certain joints which are at risk of coming apart or dislocating, due to the patterns of movement involved in the sport. Examples of supports include bandages, strappings or lightweight plastic shields on the shoulders, elbows, wrists, knees and ankles.

Warm-up exercises show if any strapping or support is needed.

Where bones meet

A joint is a structure where two bones meet. Not all joints are flexible, allowing the bones to move in relation to each other. In some parts, such as the skull, the individual bones are firmly linked, as if glued together. In other parts, such as the arms and legs, there are synovial joints which allow various amounts and directions of movements.

Fontanelles (gaps) in young skull

Sutures (firm joints) in adult skull

The bones of a baby's skull (top) gradually grow together at suture joints during childhood (above).

FIXED JOINTS

The skull seems like one bone, but it is really made up of 21 bones, fixed to each other by rigid joins called suture joints. In a suture joint, tough fibres grow between the bones, along their edges, then gradually shrink to pull the bones closer together. The fibres also become hardened by minerals, almost like real bone. This whole process takes a year or two. A newborn baby's skull bones have not quite locked solid, and there are gaps between, called fontanelles, which the bones grow into and fill. This structure allows the baby's head to squeeze slightly smaller as it emerges from the womb along the narrow birth canal.

FLEXIBLE JOINTS

In a synovial joint, such as the shoulder, the ends of the bones are covered with smooth, shiny, slightly soft cartilage. This allows the bones to slide past each other without wear. A tough synovial capsule surrounds the joint like a bag. Its lining makes slippery synovial fluid.

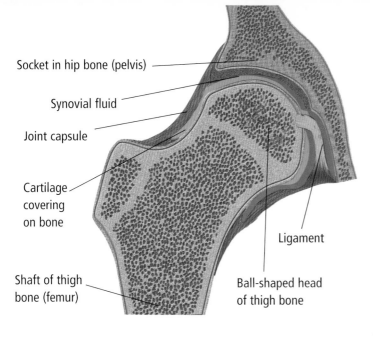

Socket in hip bone (pelvis)

Synovial fluid

Joint capsule

Cartilage covering on bone

Shaft of thigh bone (femur)

Ligament

Ball-shaped head of thigh bone

These views show the inside of the hip joint (left) and the ligaments and other coverings (below).

Hip bone (pelvis)

Ilio-femoral ligament

Pubo-femoral ligament

Shaft of thigh bone (femur)

Synovial fluid works like lubricating oil in a car's engine, so that the joint can move smoothly without rubbing or friction.

LIGAMENTS

In a flexible joint, such as the knee, the bones are held near each other by strong, slightly elastic, strap-shaped parts called ligaments. Each ligament is anchored at one end to one bone, and at the other end, to the other bone. In most joints there are several ligaments spaced out around the joint. Ligaments are strong, but they may sprain or tear under sudden strain.

Top Tips

Do warm-up exercises for muscles and joints before strenuous exercise.

Wear suitable protection to avoid excessive flexing or twisting of joints.

Treat a sprain with rest, and use an ice pack to reduce swelling.

If there is no improvement within 36–48 hours, or if the pain and stiffness are severe or worsen, always consult a doctor.

Elbow and knee pads protect these joints from hard knocks and falls.

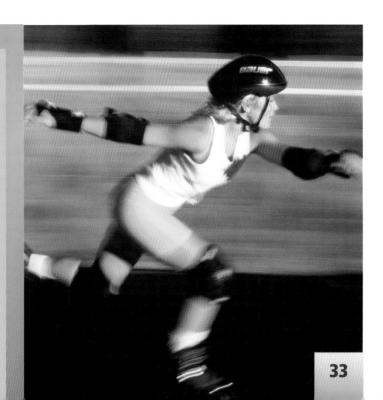

KEEPING JOINTS HEALTHY

ALLOWING MOVEMENT

Each joint's design allows a certain range of movement. The ball-and-socket design, such as the hip or shoulder, permits great flexibility but little twisting (rotation of the bone). In the back, each gliding-pivot joint includes a pad of cartilage, the intervertebral disc, which is like a cushion between the individual backbones (vertebrae). The joint can flex and twist only slightly, but over the whole backbone this adds up to considerable movement.

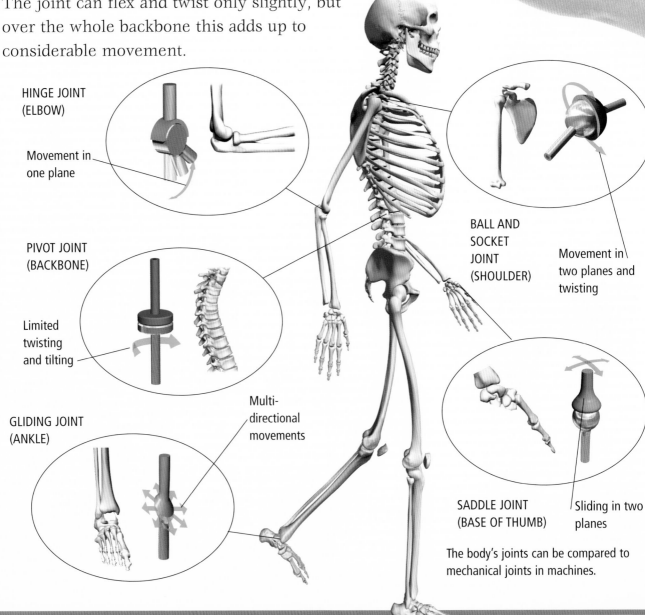

HINGE JOINT
(ELBOW)

Movement in
one plane

PIVOT JOINT
(BACKBONE)

Limited
twisting
and tilting

GLIDING JOINT
(ANKLE)

Multi-
directional
movements

BALL AND
SOCKET
JOINT
(SHOULDER)

Movement in
two planes and
twisting

SADDLE JOINT
(BASE OF THUMB)

Sliding in two
planes

The body's joints can be compared to mechanical joints in machines.

HEALTHY JOINTS

The joints of a young person are more flexible than those of an older person. But old age does not always mean stiff, aching joints. Varied activities and exercises – especially those which are physically not too stressful, like brisk walking, swimming and yoga – can keep the joints healthy and supple for many years. Sudden twists and turns, where great strain is put on joints, should generally be avoided.

Gymnasts follow special training routines to keep their muscles strong and joints supple.

ANIMAL VERSUS HUMAN

Some snakes have more than 200 vertebrae, or individual backbones. So they are very flexible and bendy, compared to a human, with 26 backbones. Some animals have far fewer vertebrae – most frogs have only eight.

A snake's backbone can coil around many times.

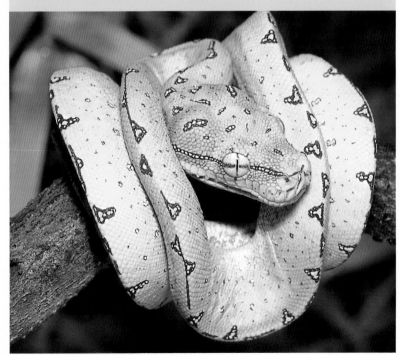

HOW THE HAND WORKS

Amazing tools

Our hands and fingers are amazing tools. They can grip and squeeze tightly, spread out wide to rub and stroke, and make the tiniest movements to pick up a pin. This is made possible by their many small bones, joints and muscles. The wrist has eight bones, known as carpals. The palm has five, called metacarpals. And there are three small bones in each finger and two in the thumb, all known as phalanges.

Fourth interosseus

Extensor muscle tendons pass through wrist

Phalanges bones of fingers

Knuckle joint

Tendon of extensor muscle in forearm

Tendon joins to thump tip

First interosseus

Flexor muscles in forearm

Abductor pollicis brevis

Sets of small muscles give fine control of hand and finger movements.

MOVING THE HAND

Each hand contains about 15 small muscles that move the thumb and fingers at their joints, called knuckles. In particular, they waggle the fingers from side to side at their knuckle joints with the palm. There are also six large muscles in the forearm which move the fingers. They have very long tendons that pass through the wrist and join to the fingers along their length. These mainly bend and straighten the fingers.

PRECISION AND POWER

The human hand is so useful, partly because it has a thumb. This can 'oppose' the fingers, when the tip of the thumb touches the tip of each finger in turn. No animal can do this. It gives us the precision grip to pick up something as small as a grain of rice very delicately, using the thumb and any other finger. It can also create the power grip, where the thumb and fingers wrap around each side of an object, such as when holding a tumbler.

An X-ray of an adult human wrist and hand shows the carpal (wrist), metacarpal (palm) and phalanges (finger) bones.

ANIMAL VERSUS HUMAN

An orang-utan has very long fingers but a short thumb. It can only hold with a hook-like grip. It hangs from its hands as it swings through the trees.

The orang-utan's hook-like hand and small thumb.

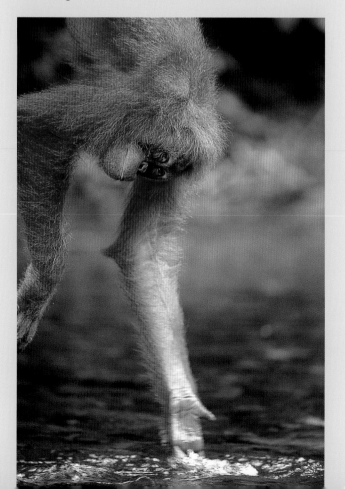

Top Tips

Muscles that are used too much or too suddenly, get tired or fatigued. They become weak and begin to shake. In the hand, this makes delicate movements difficult. Practice usually helps, as does taking a break to relax, stretch and move the fingers in other directions.

A range of movements

There are only three bones in the arm – the humerus in the upper part, and the radius and ulna which lie alongside each other in the lower part or forearm. Yet the arm can reach up, forwards, down and even around the back. This is due mainly to the very wide range of motion at the shoulder joint, the more limited bending of the elbow, and also 'rotation'. This happens when bones twist or rotate. The wrist may seem very flexible because the hand can bend forwards and backwards, and also twist around almost in a circle. In fact, the twisting happens all along the arm (see panel).

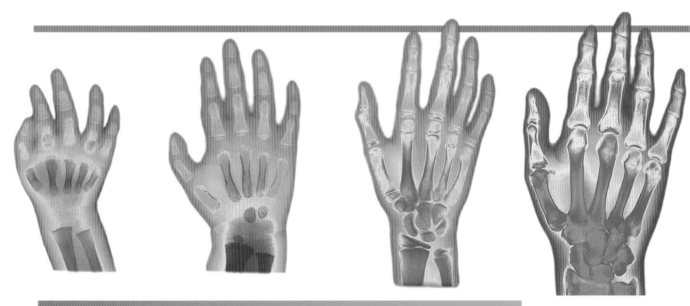

Try this!

Hold your arm out straight in front, palm up. Twist it so the palm turns to face down. Keep going and see how the hand can turn almost in a full circle, so the palm nearly faces upwards again. Now, do this while holding your forearm firmly, halfway along, with your other hand. The palm turns much less, because the only twisting motion is at the wrist. In the first case, the whole arm was involved, as its long bones twisted along their lengths.

This series of X-ray pictures shows a baby's hand growing into an adult hand. The skeleton in the wrist and hand forms first as cartilage and gradually hardens into bone, coloured blue. (See also page 37.)

FLEXIBLE VERSUS STABLE

The shoulder is a ball-and-socket synovial joint (see page 34). The ball-shaped upper end of the humerus bone fits into a bowl-shaped socket formed by the shoulder blade and collar bone. This socket is quite flat or shallow, to allow the arm its amazingly wide range of movements. But the benefit of being more flexible has a drawback – being less stable.

The shoulder's exceptional range of movement is shown well during gymnastic exercises such as the rings.

This means the shoulder joint is sometimes damaged or even pulled apart by too much sudden force, which is called dislocation.

weblinks
To find out more about the shoulder, go to:
www.waylinks.co.uk/series/ourbodies/skelandmus

Supraspinatus

Pectoralis minor

Coraco-brachialis

FRONT VIEW   BACK VIEW

Intercostals (between ribs)

Teres major

Brachialis

Brachioradialis

Supraspinatus

Deltoid

Infraspinatus

Triceps brachi

The shoulder and elbow have many sets of muscles.

THE LEG AND FOOT

Differently designed

The leg and foot have almost the same number of bones and muscles as the arm and hand. But they are designed less for being flexible, and more for carrying the body's weight. The hip is a ball-and-socket synovial joint, like the shoulder. But the bowl-like socket is deeper than the socket in the shoulder. This means the leg has a smaller range of movements than the arm. However the hip joint is much stronger and more stable or secure, and less likely to dislocate (come apart).

The power of the leg muscles can propel the whole body more than two metres off the ground, as when high-jumping.

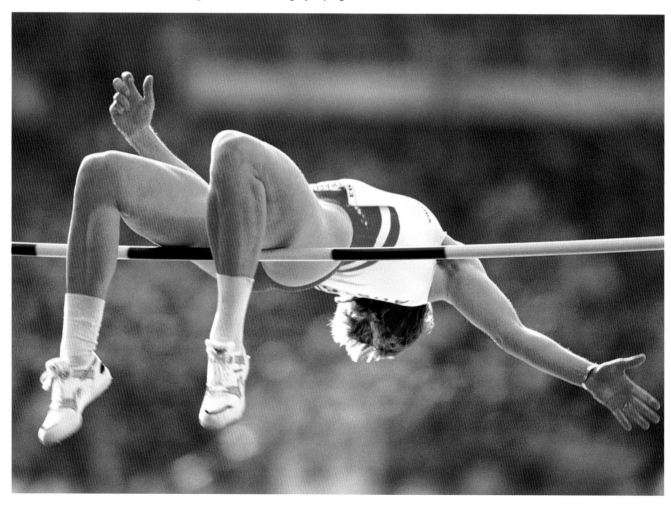

BIG AND UNUSUAL

The biggest single joint in the body is the knee. It is unusual in two ways. It has ligaments inside it, as well as around it. There are two inner ligaments between the bones, called the cruciate ligaments because they form a cross or X shape. The knee also has two extra cushion-like pieces of cartilage which 'float' in the joint, between the bone ends. These are crescent- or moon-shaped and called menisci. People such as football players and skiers who move quickly and then stop, and twist and turn at speed, put great strain on their knees. They may suffer 'cruciate trouble' or 'cartilage (meniscus) problems'. The hip and leg also have the body's largest muscle. This is the gluteus maximus, which forms part of the buttock. It pulls the thigh back as we jump and leap.

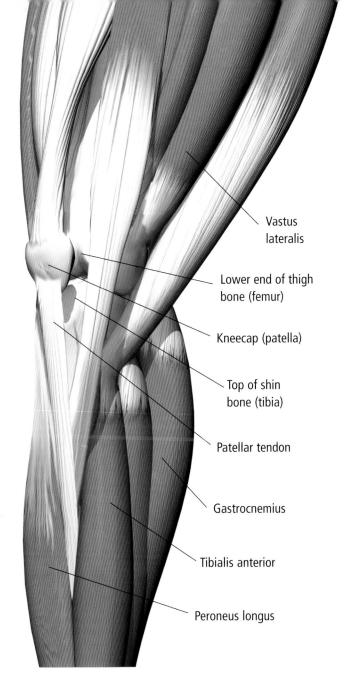

Vastus lateralis

Lower end of thigh bone (femur)

Kneecap (patella)

Top of shin bone (tibia)

Patellar tendon

Gastrocnemius

Tibialis anterior

Peroneus longus

Top Tips

Cramp is very painful tensing or contraction of a muscle, which feels hard and 'knotted'. Cramp tends to affect muscles which are used suddenly after long periods of inactivity. The remedy is to stretch the muscle gently by moving the body part, and massage it. However medical advice is needed for cramps that occur frequently or continue for long periods.

In the knee, the rounded knuckle-like lower end of the femur (thigh bone) fits into the slightly dished top of the tibia (shin bone). The kneecap or patella is an unusual bone because it is entirely inside a large tendon, called the patellar tendon. It protects the knee joint at the front.

BACK JOINTS AND MUSCLES

A tower of strength

The backbone or spine is the main 'girder' or 'tower' of the body, holding up the head, arms and torso (central body). It is not one bone, but a chain-like row of 26 bones known as vertebrae. There are seven vertebrae in the neck region, 12 in the chest (each one joined to a pair of ribs), five in the lower back, one in the hip region joined to the hip bones, and one small 'tail' bone at the lower end. A tunnel runs through the whole backbone. Inside it, well protected, is the body's main nerve – the spinal cord.

BACK MUSCLES

Each vertebra has long rod-like extensions called neural spines or processes. These are anchor points where muscles are attached. About 25 sets of long, slim muscles run up and down the backbone, overlapping each other. They join to different sets of vertebrae, and link the backbone to the head, shoulders, ribs and hips. These vertebral muscles give the whole backbone great strength. They also hold the shoulders and hips steady as the arms and legs move.

Semispinalis cervicis

Semispinalis capitis

Longissimus

Spinalis

Quadratus lumborum

Sets of long back muscles hold the back upright when standing, and allow it to bend and twist. The cartilage pad or disc, between each pair of bones in the back, is very strong and tough. It has an outer layer made of stringy fibres, and a slightly more flexible inner layer, or centre, almost like stiff jelly.

JOINTS IN THE BACK

The vertebral bones have specialized joints. Each has a pad of cartilage between its two vertebrae, that works like a cushion to absorb knocks and jolts, and to let the bones move and tilt slightly. The pad is called the intervertebral disc (see page 34). The disc and the joint's structure allow the two bones to move only slightly in relation to each other. But along the whole backbone, these small movements add up, so the back can bend almost 'double' in a U shape.

A neck injury may be very serious, because of the risk of damage to the spinal cord, which carries nerve signals between brain and body. A neck guard or stabilizer is carefully fitted to hold and support the head during transport to hospital or medical centre.

Try this!

Stand up straight, then slowly and carefully, bend your back to the front, side and rearwards. (Do not strain it.) Which direction is easiest and most flexible? The joints between the vertebrae also allow twisting, so you can keep your feet still, but turn around so your head can look backwards.

JOINT PROBLEMS

Back strain

Everyday actions such as walking, jogging and correct lifting rarely strain the joints. One exception is the back. A back strain is more likely if a person lifts a heavy load by leaning over and bending the back, and perhaps twisting as well, rather than by bending at the hips and knees. Sometimes one of the pads or discs between two backbones gets squeezed so much, it bulges at a weak point in its outer layer and presses on a nearby nerve, causing great pain. The bulge is called a prolapsed (or 'slipped') disc.

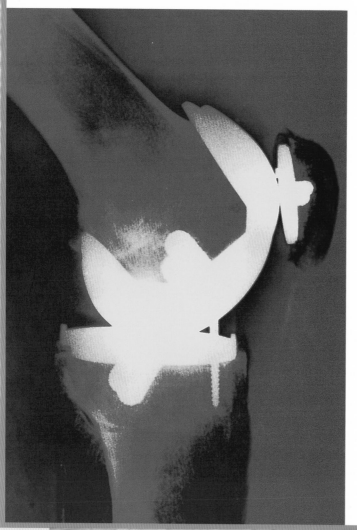

ARTHRITIS

The scientific name for a joint is an arthrosis. The main problems which affect joints, producing pain and swelling, are known as arthritis. There are several types. In osteoarthritis a joint becomes worn, and in particular, the smooth cartilage in the joint becomes rough and flaky. This is made more likely by old age, too much strain on the joints over the years, and previous injuries. The joints are stiff and aching, especially in the morning after a night's rest.

Many types of artificial joints, such as this knee, are based on the design of the real joint within the body, and allow a similar range of movements.

SELF-ATTACK

Rheumatoid arthritis is a complicated disease where the body's immune system, which is supposed to attack invading germs, mistakenly attacks parts of the body itself. This is known as an auto-immune problem. The attacked joints become swollen, painful, stiff and deformed with lumps. In younger people rheumatoid arthritis is more common compared to osteoarthritis, but it is still a rare condition.

TREATMENTS

Many kinds of medicinal drugs can help different forms of arthritis. So can an operation, either to treat the affected parts, or to replace them with an artificial joint made of special, hard-wearing plastic and metal.

HEALTHY MUSCLES AND BONES

The body's musculo-skeletal system is designed for movement and activity. But unsuitable activity and excessive strain can lead to problems – as can under-use of the system due to inactivity.

Experts such as sports coaches and exercise leaders can give advice about keeping the right balance.

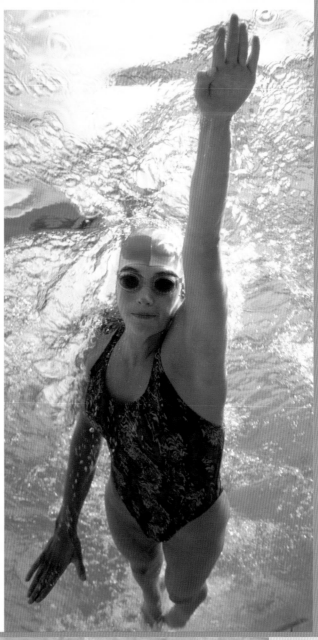

weblinks
To find out more about joint problems, go to:
www.waylinks.co.uk/series/ourbodies/skelandmus

Swimming allows the body to be active while supported by water.

MICRO-BODY

The cartilage in a joint affected by osteoarthritis is rough, pitted and crumbly, rather than smooth and slightly bendy.

GLOSSARY

actin One of the two main substances shaped as long, thin filaments which, with myosin, is grouped in bundles to form a muscle fibril, and which slides past filaments of myosin to make a muscle contract.

antagonistic To work against or oppose, as in antagonistic muscle partners attached to one bone, which pull the bone in different or opposite ways.

bone marrow A soft, jelly-like substance in the middle of some bones.

calcium An important mineral for the body, which in crystal form gives strength and hardness to bones and teeth, and also keeps other parts of the body, such as nerves, healthy.

cancellous (spongy) bone A fairly strong but also lightweight, honeycomb-type of bone, which forms the middle layer of most bones.

cardiac muscle The type of muscle that forms the walls of the heart.

cartilage A strong, tough, lightweight, fairly stiff but slightly bendy substance, that makes up structural parts of the body such as inside the nose and ears, and which also covers the ends of bones in most types of joints.

cell A single unit or 'building block' of life – the human body is made of billions of cells of many different kinds.

collagen An important structural substance in the body – a protein made of many tiny, strong, tough fibres that occurs in the skin, tendons and many other parts of the body.

compact (hard) bone A strong, hard, dense type of bone, which forms the outer layer or 'shell' of most bones, around the less strong cancellous (spongy) layer.

contract In a muscle, when it tenses and pulls and becomes shorter.

hormones Natural body chemicals made by parts called endocrine glands, that circulate in blood and control many processes such as growth, the use of energy, water balance and the formation of urine.

involuntary muscles See visceral muscles.

ligament A strong, slightly stretchy, usually strap-shaped part, that holds two bones together at a joint to limit their movements and stop them coming apart.

marrow See bone marrow.

muscle fibres Long, thin, thread-shaped parts (myofibres) that are grouped in bundles to make up the bulk of a muscle.

muscle fibrils Long, thin, thread-shaped parts (myofibrils) that are grouped in bundles to make up the bulk of a muscle fibre.

myofibre See muscle fibres.

myofibril See muscle fibrils.

myosin One of the two main substances shaped as long, thin filaments which, with actin, is grouped in bundles to form a muscle fibril, and which slides past filaments of actin to make a muscle contract.

oxygen A gas making up one-fifth of air, which has no colour, taste or smell, but which is vital for breaking down nutrients inside the body to obtain energy for life processes.

peristalsis The wave-like, squeezing motion of muscles, especially where they form a tube or bag and squeeze to move along the contents.

phosphate A mineral made from the substances phosphorus and oxygen, which in crystal form gives strength and hardness to bones and teeth.

relax In a muscle, when it is no longer tense and pulling, but becomes floppy and can be pulled longer or stretched.

skeletal muscles Types of muscles which are mostly joined to the bones of the skeleton, and which are voluntary, able to be moved at will (rather than working automatically without conscious will), and which have tiny stripes or striations when seen under the microscope.

skeleton All of the body's bones and also the supporting parts made of cartilage, or 'gristle'.

smooth muscles See visceral muscles.

striped muscles See skeletal muscles.

tendon A very strong, tough, fibrous, rope-like part, where a muscle tapers thinner and anchors to a bone or to another muscle.

visceral muscles Types of muscles which are mostly deep within the body, especially in the chest and abdomen, but are not joined to the bones of the skeleton, and which are involuntary (working automatically without conscious will), and which look 'smooth' under the microscope because they lack tiny stripes or striations.

vitamins The naturally-occurring substances either made by the body or taken up in food, which are needed to keep the body healthy and avoid illness.

voluntary muscles See skeletal muscles.

BOOKS

Bones and Muscles, Suzanne Levert (Benchmark Books, 2001)

The Skeleton and Movement, Steve Parker (Franklin Watts Inc, 1999)

Bones, Carol Ballard (Heinemann Library, 2003)

The Skeleton and Muscular System, Carol Ballard, Steve Parker (Raintree Steck Vaughn, 1997)

ORGANIZATIONS

Muscular Dystrophy Campaign
A UK charity focusing on all muscular dystrophies and allied disorders, which has pioneered the search for treatments and cures for over 40 years and provides support to people affected by the condition.
7–11 Prescott Place, London SW4 6BS
Tel: 020 7720 8055

National Osteoporosis Society
The only national UK charity dedicated to improving the diagnosis, prevention and treatment of this fragile bone disease.
Camerton, Bath BA2 0PJ   Tel: 01761 471771

Arthritis Care
The UK's largest voluntary organization working with and for people with arthritis.
18 Stephenson Way, London NW1 2HD
Tel: 020 7380 6500

BackCare
Registered as National Back Pain Association (Charity No.256751)
The charity for healthier backs is dedicated to educating people on how to avoid preventable back pain, and supporting those living with back pain.
16 Elmtree Road, Teddington
Middlesex, TW11 8ST
Tel: 020 8977 5474

INDEX